Oberammergau

OBERAMMERGAU

The village of the Passion Play and its surroundings

PUBLISHED BY LUDWIG SIMON VERLAG

MUNICH-PULLACH

The Crucifixion Group on the Osterbichl-mountain near Oberammergau, founded by the Bavarian King Ludwig II in 1875, is in its simple sublimity in connection with the surrounding nature like a symbol of the Passion-Play-Village. As the inscription of the monument says, it is devoted "To the inhabitants of Oberammergau who love the art and are faithful to the customs of their ancestors."

The visitor of Oberammergau entering this country near Eschenlohe is offered the first welcome from the rocky summit of the Ettaler Mandl, a greeting full of mountain air and heartiness.

The Passion-Play-Village Oberammergau and its surrounding country

By Erika Schwarz. - Translation by Trude Zettlitz

Oberammergau! — This word sounds solemnly like a bell that swings in the pure blue morning. The longer it sounds the more powerful becomes its tune sounding far over hills and mountains, forests and meadows. The silverwaves of the Ammer-river carry it away, the winds lift it up, the clouds take it with them as a light burden.

Oberammergau — doesn't the bell sound through the wide country, even through the whole world?

The Passion-Play-Village, protected by the surrounding mountains, is situated in a circular valley through which the Ammer-river flows. The peculiarly shaped Kofel-peak puts itself prominently into the foreground.

It seems like the time has never been more fugitive than it is now. It is harrassing and hasting, pushing the people with it. But, suddenly, there is something in its way that has been and will be, that has saved its persistence and validity through all the storm and stress. The people grasp after the old values with a sudden understanding of the things that are true and permanent. Do we count Oberammergau among the values and deeds of everlasting validity? In 1633 a vow was made and in more than 300 years the passionsplays have been performed every ten years. The people who were coming to the "Passion", have increased from time to time, first there were hundreds of them, later thousands, and now there are hundredthousands. There are

Typical street of Oberammergau: a neat Upperbavarian village, spick and span, idyllic and rustical, whith mountains in the background; but also a famous place which is looked upon by the world.

some of them coming only in order to have been present, but there will hardly be one who would leave without being under a deep impression.

The essential thing comes from the deep faith of the play. In addition there are other powers to make the "Passion" what it is: that is the village of Oberammergau, this lovely place in the mountains, that is the atmosphere of the tradition; the theater; the artistic craftsmanship; talented and artistically gifted people; and last but not least the mountain scenery. In all directions this scenery is a beautiful frame.

Oberammergau is the center of a widely spread territory. Yet the mixture of the dialects proves that to

The different picturesque streets are like a stage: the daily life provides the actors, the houses and streets like side-scenes shifted into each other; and in the background a view of the mountains.

be true. For here the sound of the Bavarian dialect shows the influence of the Tyrol and the Swabian-Alemanic accent. From all sides different expressions are combined and form a whole that is original, picturesque and full of feeling. And as the language is keeping together the three sections, so does the landscape. In the western part the silhouettes of the Allgäu are seen clearly and distinctly. These are very impressive and peculiarly shaped peaks. Towards the south the landscape changes to the more gigantic mountains of Tyrol. In the east it is connected with the Loisach-valley and the Werdenfels country. To the north stretches a chain of Bavarian mountains.

9

Originally the plays took place in the churchyard, later on in the "Passion-Meadow" until 1830. The present building which was constructed in 1930 holds more than 5000 persons in its large auditorium.

Such influences are at all times fertile and beneficial, for they stimulate and inspire the people. So we find here an active, energetic mountain-tribe. These people are much less reserved than the people in other parts of the Alps, they are more kindly disposed and affable and their artistic talents are eye-catching. Only a people favored by the muses may preserve a play through centuries. Not the vow and the conscience are the only maintaining powers; there is in the same measure the artistic element that is characteristic for the Bavarian and the Alemanic tribe. Like the painters of the Renaissance and the Baroque, choosing religious motives and making them the subject of their art, it is here that the religious, Christian theater keeps the people in suspense,

The church is the center of the village. Oberammergau counts half a million visitors at the time of the passionplay. The play has grown beyond the local miracle-play, it has become the play of the whole world.

the magic of the spoken word, the charm of the gesture and metamorphosis, the apotheosis of the music. In addition to this comes the other artistic element: the art of woodcarving. It is assumed that it originated from the monastery of Rottenbuch. The monasteries were the first supporters of civilization. The monks in addition to teaching agriculture, cattle-breeding and trades also tought reading, writing and artistic skills. Both Oberammergau and Berchtesgaden may owe the monks of Rottenbuch a great debt of gratitude for giving them the art of carving for it was the monks of Rottenbuch who, as pioneers of faith and culture, came to the woodlands of Berchtesgaden and Oberammergau. From these circumstances a common origin may be

Quaint houses, often decorated whith rich ornaments, make Oberammergau so unique. The above shown Klepperhaus is the original house of the Lang-family, famous as a family of actors and woodware-dealers.

concluded. However, the development of the art of woodcarving went into different directions. Berchtesgaden being more concentrated on the production of toys, boxes and utensils for common use, the masters of Oberammergau devoted themselves more and more to the woodcarving of pictures and religious figures. Out of the simple relief-technic, mostly serving for decorative purposes, the full-plastic shaping of figures was developed. Religious motives were predominating. Woodcarvings of cribs and passion motives are dating back as far as to the time of the Gothic style. In former centuries the woodcarving was of greater importance than it is today. Oberammergau has been faithful to its woodcarving continuously. It was and is the main

A little preciousness is the "Lueftlmaler-Haus" (Fresco-Painter-House). Between richly adorned window-frames and doorposts gaily colored frescos are interspersed, heaven-inspired ideas of the fresco-painter Franz Zwink.

source of the population's income. Agents were mediating the sale of the goods produced. Their connections went far to foreign countries and there existed tight commercial links with Venice, Cadix and Amsterdam. In Bavaria the goods were sold by peddlers who carried them in a porter's strap. The Oberammergau woodcarvers of crucifixes became famous and gained great esteem. Here the Passion may again have its influence. Through the deep emotions for the play the crucified Christ became a symbol of their art. Now there is in Oberammergau a training school for woodcarving and a great number of workshops. The religious motive of Christ is not the only pattern but is a symbol of the art of woodcarving.

The inn "Zum Weißen Lamm" (At the White Lamb) is the birthplace of the teacher Rochus Dedler, one of the three companion stars: Father Weiß, who rewrote the text of the passionplay, Father Daisenberger, the editor, and Rochus Dedler, the composer.

Oberammergau is situated at the place where the Ammer-river, the murmuring mountain stream, is leaving the mountains. The valley becomes wider and wider and towards the north the highland is changing into hills and swellings. There is a railway connection from Murnau that has to surmount remarkable slopes, and a narrow road with many curves, always ascending and descending. The main auto highway is from Garmisch-Oberau in the southeast to Füssen in the west. It is a convenient road in a changing scenery.

The Kofel-peak is the symbol of Oberammergau. Though not being extremely high it is a mountain with

At the time of the passionplay Oberammergau becomes almost city-like. In both summer and winter it is an attractive place for tourists, falling back into rustic simplicity. It is always inviting and full of hospitality.

an absolute characteristic shape, capriciously and proudly raising its rocky nose out of a green forest coat. It seems bold and important.

The Hörnle-mountain and Laber-mountain at the eastern side are inviting mountains to visit in each season. They make the visit easy and present their guests a view that reaches from the silver-blue mirror of the many lakes as far as to the snowcovered peak of the Zugspitze. The Ettaler Manndl, the boldly raised rock, belongs to this kind mountain group. To ascend it has become easier by well secured climbing facilities. In the west there is the main range of the Ammergau mountains. The Kolbenalm, easily reached by a lift, opens

One of the most beautiful houses of the village is the "Pilatushaus" so called because the main fresco shows Christ with Pilatus. Here a climax of baroque house-painting is reached.

the way to the Pürschling-mountain, to the Sonnenbergspitze and Teufelstättkopf. Further mountain tours are to the Laubeneck and to the Hennenkopf and Brunnenkopfhouses, the Klammspitze and then follows the Hochplatte that already leads over to the territory of the Lech-river. These Ammergau mountains are varied, accessible and frequently visited. Good ways, marked paths and sheltering huts help the touristic traffic. The sunny pastures give the mountainous country an idyllic and lovely charm. In the south a third range of mountains appears, the eastern part rising from the Loisach-valley, the western part descending to the Ammerforest, beautiful lonely mountains, peacefully stretched in front of the Wetterstein mountains. Silent woods

Wherever you go, the mountains dominate the scenery. Above all is the Kofel mountain towering behind the village. It is the first peak in the Ammergau mountain chain which reaches as far as Füssen.

vary with remote pastures. Among dwarf-pines blossoms the alpine rose, in the lonely highvalley yells the whistling of the marmots, in the rocks the alpine goats are bustling about. The huge forest has a wonderful, healthy stock of deer being one of the best red game stocks of the whole Bavarian Alps. This territory was the favored hunting ground of Bavarian monarchs and today it is a territory under preservation of natural beauty.

The names of the mountains are: Notkarspitze, to be reached on a hunting path from Graswang or Ettal, there behind the Brünstlskopf, Vorderer Felderkopf and Windstierlkopf, then the wide-spread Frieder, a separate mountain group, and the Kuchelberg. The highest peak is the Kreuzspitze which offers a wonderful

The most beautiful and widest view of the valley and the lovely situated village is from
the surrounding mountains as the above picture, taken from the Osterbichl-peak, or

view. The Little Kreuzspitze, approximately two thousand meters high, is easier to reach; it also gives the

magnificent view to the Eibsee.

The most beautiful view to the village of Oberammergau is from the Osterbichl-mountain on which the

Crucifixion Group was erected, a gift by Ludwig II to the Passion Play Village. It is really a beautiful village

of delightful Bavarian character. How lovely it is situated in the valley with its shimmering river! The houses

with their flat gables, far projecting roofs and balconies are richly decorated with paintings. From the time

around the year of 1800 there are the famous mural paintings by Franz Zwink whose great artistic creative

this picture, taken from the Kolbensattel-mountain, shows. The situation between the Werdenfels country and the Allgäu favored its development. It has become the link between these two places of the Bavarian tourist traffic.

power changed blank fronts of houses into deligthful fresco-paintings. He was called the "Lüftlmaler" because he did his paintings with an amazing speed. The story says that he once made a bet with a farmer's wife that he will have his paintings sooner finished than she will have finished stirring the butter — and indeed, he had won the bet — whereby certainly the gay picture was a higher prize than the piece of butter!

The church, from the outside like any other of the many towered whitewashed Bavarian village churches, shows in its interior a festival hall with stucco-work, golden and adorned with statues of saints, able to compete with the brilliant churches in the vicinity.

19

The valley of Graswang branches off near Oberammergau. From the top of the Pürschling-peak there is a panorama of its beauty. The castle Linderhof nestled in the distance, is the main attraction there.

A point of attraction is the museum with its woodcarvings, the workshops and the appertaining shops. Not to forget the comfortable guest houses uniting the homely and rustic features with the comfort of modern facilities.

The Festival Hall is a tremendous building. From the roofed auditorium one looks into the open air. The sky is arching above the Passionplay, the background are the mountains.

On the eastern side of the village is the massive building of the Passion Play Theater with its roofed auditorium, the simple open-air-style stage whose last and greatest background are the mountains.

View of the interior of the Pfarrkirche. The exterior of the church does not disclose anything of the magnificent hall decorated in Rococo style. The church was constructed in the middle of the 18th century.

After the invasion of the Swedes had been overcome in 1632, the black plague raging in Garmisch, in Partenkirchen, in Eschenlohe, everywhere death holding harvest, the people of Oberammergau wanted to protect their village from the plague and a strict order was issued that no one from outside was allowed to enter the village. They believed this prevention would help and they posted guards around the village. One night, a farmhelp from Eschenlohe being very anxious about his family who were living in Ammergau, sneaked across the mountains into his native village. At the door of his house he collapsed and died. The next day the plague came over the village. It cut the people off, one after the other, and there was great distress. Thus the

The increased sentiment for space goes into ecstasy in the monastery-church of Ettal. In devotional glory the cupola is arching, decorated by a dramatic fresco rich in colors and figures.

town council decided to make a vow to perform the passionplay every ten years. Since that time no one died from the plague.

In the following year of 1633 the play was performed for the first time. Thereafter it was to take place every decade. All times the people of the village were eager to fulfill the vow although it was often very difficult because of wars, economical catastrophies and prohibitions.

In the 19th century the play was reformed as to its text and music by Father Ottmar from Ettal, the teacher Dedler and the chaplain Daisenberger from Oberammergau. Its final styling was by these three

Like a dream, cupolas and towers of the monastery Ettal arise out of the mountain scenery. Legend and romance weave around its foundation. Through all times the Benedictine-Abbey enjoyed good reputation and esteem.

men. The actors are solely natives of Oberammergau and every person taking part is a member of the community.

Always lives Oberammergau under the symbol of the Passion, including those years when there are no performances. And there is the question: are the people of Oberammergau a special tribe or did the tradition, the passion for acting, create in them the characteristic features of Christ, Petrus and Pilatus. Important days are the ones when the casting of the parts takes place. Then the whole village is waiting for the results in front of the townhall. Mimic talents are not solely the decisive factor, for the dignity of the play demands also a

In its whole architecture, especially in its monastery-church, the Ettal monastery is a unique building, a perfect fusion of High-Gothic and Rococo style. Many famous artists have worked on its completion.

blameless moral conduct of the actor-to-be. Hair and beards must be grown and so it happens that one or two years before the passionplay a bearded, long-haired man attracts the attention here and there between Munich and Garmisch-Partenkirchen. He is one of the passionplayers of Oberammergau.

In summertime Oberammergau is a health resort offering various possibilities for recreation. It is the beautiful valley, the mountains, the vicinity of the Royal Castles, Ettal, Garmisch-Partenkirchen, and the Staffelsee that makes Oberammergau attractive. Its reputation as a winter resort is founded on the Pürschling and Laber mountains and its reliable snow conditions. At the time of the passionplay, the whole world is

Once more let's take a look at the Passion-Play-Village and then we will get acquainted with some others of the sights which Upper-Bavaria offers its visitors of the passionplay.

meeting here: colors, languages, a variety of people. But the village does not loose its characteristic features, it remains Oberammergau, the Passion Play Village.

Oberammergau is not an arbitrary or incidental settlement but it grew out of a Roman fort at the great military road and trade route from Venice across the Brenner Pass via Innsbruck, Scharnitz, Partenkirchen to Augsburg. The fort at the exit of the mountains lost its importance with the decay of the Roman power.

History tells of a duke of the Guelphs who resided in the castle of Ambrigow (Middle High German for

Towards the north there is an ancient civilized country, rather known as the Pfaffenwinkel (Cleric Corner). From its highest hill, the Hohenpeißenberg, one has a wide view of the Ammergau country.

Oberammergau). The village developed from the early-medievial settlement around the castle. It did not gain any prestige or prosperity until the great commercial towns on this side and beyond the Alps grew up. Jewelery, silk, wine from the south, spices from the orient, furs and handmade products from the north — the streets of these towns were full of life and the villages grew. Post offices, inns, warehouses, craftshops, everything was welcome and cheap. Also Oberammergau was developing during this time. Its importance in the middle ages was considerable because of its situation between the commercial town of Füssen and the industrious Parten-kirchen which was named "Golden Country". Oberammergau has close connections with the village of Ettal

The Eibsee at the foot of the massive steep-sides of the Wetterstein-mountains. Water
and rocks are increasing to a unique effect which is most impressive in the evening light

when the setting sun throws its light on the rocks. Behind the Eibsee-Hotel is the station of the Zugspitz-railway which from here ascends to the summit of the Zugspitze.

Both in summer and in winter the Pürschling-Houses are a frequently visited touristic point. They promise the enjoyment of all mountain beauty: a magnificent view and, in winter, thrilling tobogganing or enjoyful skiing.

in the neighborhood. This village is famous for its monastery. The monastery-church of Ettal is considered to be one of the most perfect buildings of the Rococo, the construction of the interior as a rotunda is over-whelming, impressive but in every respect it keeps the measure of spirituality and nobleness. It does not dissolve in glorification but it ends in golden ornamented elegance. History and legend merge into each other and bind a romantic wreath around its foundation, dating back to the days of Ludwig the Bavarian. It is said that the emperor had received a painting of St. Mary, with the order to find a dignified place for it. Therefore he was promised help in his bad need of money. Strange things happened near Ettal when Ludwig was riding home

A quiet place of peace and meditation is the Kalvarienberg (Mount Calvary) near Eschenlohe. The village, situated at the foot of the mountains, offers the tourists hospitality on the way to Oberammergau.

from Italy across the Alps. A version of the legend says that the painting of St. Mary became more and more heavy till it pressed his horse down to the earth. The other version says the horse fell three times on its knees to show that the selected place was found. In any case the emperor founded the monastery here and monks and knights came to the lonely mountain-valley to apply themselves to religious contemplations and silent devotion. Fate changed the monastery many times until it became the present outstanding educational institution. The bright colored building amidst the beauty of rustling mountain forests and green meadows is like a symbol of monastic civilizing work in the Bavarian country.

Towering above the Ammer-river, the Augustiner-convent Rottenbuch was once one of the most famous monasteries of the Pfaffenwinkel. The church in its sublime splendour is worthwhile seeing.

Near Oberammergau the highway to Garmisch branches off to Linderhof castle. The level road leads
into a long valley, surrounded by mountains, meadows and forests, passing through the little village of Gras-

A hymn of beauty is the Wies-church, situated in the scenery of the spurs of the Alps. The most beautiful Rococo-church in all the country — not solely a shrine for pious pilgrims but also for all those who seek and love beauty.

wang, cut off from the world, and then to the royal castle Linderhof. A castle in quiet loneliness amidst green meadows and woods, a castle with magnificent gardens, with stylish flights of stairs and sparkling fountains,

Above the lovely Alpsee is the castle Hohenschwangau, once the residence of the nobles of Schwangau, later a ruin, and finally reconstructed by kings, who were fond of building. Today it belongs

basins and grottos, with arboured walks and hedge-rows, little statues of playing angels and sweet perfume of flowers and beautiful colors. Everything is artistically arranged in steps, towering, skillfully using the slopes of the mountains, delightfully planned in all details by the famous Effner. Grand rooms with precious gobelins, with furniture of rosewood, with Malachite and Lapislazuli — a royal dream! But at last as a whole it can — like the other architecture by Ludwig II — be contested as a work of art for this king never found the sound realism of a sovereign, but became lost in phantastic imaginations and pecularities. In the restlesness of his heart he lived a solitary life. In order not to be seen or recognized by anyone, he drove under the covers of

34

to the famous "Royal Castles", of which the second one is the castle Linderhof, a magic realization of royal dreams. Murmuring fountains, beautiful flower-gardens — a gem amidst forests and mountains.

night in ghostly hurry to Linderhof, to Neuschwanstein or to one of his other castles, but not to enjoy there in rest and peace the beauty, the unique, as a maecenas of arts, a friend of science or a patron of culture. No, Ludwig fled from his unrest and tried to drown the shadows of pain and doubts with splendor and pomp. Thus only, the excessive abundance and eccentricity can be explained. But all this gives no reason to say that the Royal Castles are no sights — one must not condemn or spend too much praise where there should be an understanding for a restless lonely man.

Towards the north the way leads to Unterammergau and Bad Kohlgrub, a beautiful country, old Bavarian

Where the Lech-river forces its way through the mountains is the town of Füssen. Here Swabian gaiety is joined with Old-Bavarian uprightness. Also the visitor enjoys this cosiness everywhere in this vivid place.

farmland, blessed with a wonderful landscape and furnished with many witnesses of prosperous Bavarian culture and civilization.

The Ammer, a brisk little mountain river, makes its way to the north. Encountering many obstacles, it meanders and winds and cuts its bed deeply into the landscape. This lovely Ammer-valley is the northern foreland. Meadows and fields, leafy woods and pine woods, stately farmhouses situated on hills, villages gathered around the baroque churches, many hills rising higher and higher towards the south. In the valley the silver sparkling Ammer-river, then the migthy arch of the Eschelsbach bridge, and scattered in the landscape three

36

And here is the third royal castle, Neuschwanstein. A castle, erected high on the rocks, crenelated and with many towers. King Ludwig II was the founder. It is possible to visit all three castles on one day.

churches: Rottenbuch, Steingaden and Wies. In 1085 the first of the Bavarian Guelphs founded the monastery of Rottenbuch that gained high prosperity. The monastery of Rottenbuch was originally built in the Gothic style. In later years it was restored in the Baroque style, decorated walls with gracious Rococo ornaments. The Gothic sterness is loosened, the abundance of the conformation removes narrowness — the Heaven's grace is coming to the prayer. About one hundred years later, in 1177, Steingaden was founded as a monastery of the Praemonstratenser order. This church still has its Romanic style but shows the influence of noble Rococo style. Although the wonderful structures of Rottenbuch and Steingaden are relatively very little known, the church

The Loisach-valley is the maingate to Oberammergau. The friendly villages of the wide
pasture land have a gigantic background: the towering massive Wetterstein-mountains.

of Wies is very famous. Most impressive of this church is the harmony of architecture and nature. The peace-

ful scenery with its fresh meadows, fragrant forests and gently rising slopes, this loveliness is the frame of the

church which like a reflection of eternal glorification shines into this world. The Wies-Church, built in the

middle of the 18th century by Dominikus Zimmermann, is said to be one of the most beautiful Rococo-

churches, is likened to an angel's song in this divine architecture of the scenery.

Farther to the south, close to the border of Tyrol, opens the wide valley of Schwangau and Füssen. The

first welcome: the white church of St. Colomann, a chapel erected in the remembrance of the plague, situated

A wide view of the Werdenfels country and its mountains is offered from the Wank-mountain which can be reached by cable-car from Partenkirchen. The mighty steep mountain sides of the Karwendel-mountains are rising in the background.

in the meadows. High on a steep rock Neuschwanstein, Ludwig's knightly royal castle, was erected, painted in pale colors, with many towers and crenelated. It is the evident expression of imperial dignity and power, its interior splendid and magnificent, climaxing in a verily royal throne-room. Opposite is the castle Hohenschwangau, inherited property of the medievial counts of Schwangau who ruled the country from their high castle. Ludwig's father, Max II, had already restored the fundament of the dilapidated castle. Ludwig's task was to complete the construction and style the interior. Hohenschwangau, Neuschwanstein and Linderhof are to be considered as a whole, the three Royal Castles have become an unit and are frequented places of Upperbavaria.

Just on the point, where the Wettersteingebirge reaches its highest peaks, the world-famous resort Garmisch-Partenkirchen is situated; Both these place have their own individual charms.

Füssen is situated on the point where the Lech-river breaks foaming and roaring through the mountain gate. It is an old town, already with Alemanic features. The narrow streets and corners, the houses with the slim, high gables, the dialect and temper of the people is Swabian. In summer its picture is reflected in the brilliancy of its lakes, situated around the town. The most beautiful lake probably being the Alpsee, situated in a higher region amidst green mountains. Also very attractive is the idyllic scenery of the Weissensee. In winter Füssen favours the ice sport although its mountains offer excellent skiing conditions.

The counterbalance for the northern and western tourist attractions is the southeast. Our attention is drawn to the twin-community of Garmisch-Partenkirchen, where the highest summits of the Wetterstein

The gate to the Karwendel-mountains is Mittenwald, close to the border of Tyrol. The village has not only a beautiful rural architecture but is also very famous for its violin-makers known all over the world.

mountains tower, where the foaming rivers Partnach and Loisach are united in a wide valley surrounded by mountains. Both settlements finding the right space to expand and to develop. Today the villages are grown together and only the initiated know that the Partnach is the boundary. Elegant streets, well-kept and attractive houses, hotels, city-like restaurants, full shops, and the pulsating life, especially in Garmisch, give both places a great attraction. Exceedingly picturesque are the old parts in Partenkirchen. The famous Frühlingsstraße in Garmisch is world-known. Worthwhile seeing are also the churches and museums. Naturally most of the visitors are going to the famous sightseeing-points of the Eibsee, Badersee, Riessersee, Partnachklamm, Höllentalklamm. Numerous other excursions are offered. The most attractive points are the cable cars going up to the

The Werdenfels country offers an abundance of natural beauty. The Alpspitze, Dreitor-spitze and the Waxensteine, seen from the chapel Gerold, give an impressive picture.

Wank-mountain and Kreuzeck-mountain and the mountain railway to the Zugspitze. Towering the bustle of life, the noble rock of the Alpspitze shines like a beacon of everlasting beauty. Winter is the great season for Garmisch-Partenkirchen which has become the top German winter sports resort.

Along the Loisach-river one can find many lovely places. Leaving the mountain area it turns towards the east. The Staffelsee, the warmest of all Bavarian lakes, situated in front of the Ammer-mountains, is offering its welcome but the Loisach-river takes its course to the Kochelsee through which it is flowing. From Kochel which gave the lake its name, the Kesselberg-road leads in many curves to the Walchensee whose quietness and solemn beauty is awe inspiring. The village of Wallgau offers the view of the valley of Mittenwald. A

Farther to the east is the Walchensee. The road is leading in many curves across the Kesselberg mountain, passing by the village of Walchensee, into the upper Isar-valley, in which Mittenwald is situated.

string is sounding: Mathias Klotz discovered the hazel-pine in the forests of the Karwendel-mountains and began to make violins of its wood. In this way Klotz helped to make this mountain-village to a community of violin-makers. Mittenwald is a village of architectural beauty situated between the Karwendel-mountains.

Herewith the ring around Oberammergau is closed. Everyone may judge how strongly the Passion Play Village is holding its position as the center and how far its influence reaches. There are many things offered to the visitors and everyone will find something of special interest to himself. But all of them will leave deeply impressed as a whole.

*

Maria: Annemarie Mayr, born 1929

Apostle Petrus: Hugo Rutz sen., born 1886

Christ: Anton Preisinger, born 1912

Magdalena: Gabriele Gropper, born 1925

Kaiphas: Benedikt Stückl jun., born 1923

Ezechiel: Hermann Haser, born 1912

Judas: Hans Schwaighofer, born 1920

Franz Zwink, understudy of Christ, born 1923

The photographs were taken by:

Lala Aufsberg: Page 32, 33; Clausing: Page 46 above and below, 47 below; Johannes: Page 23; H. Kronburger: Page 17, 18, 19, 22, 44, 45, 47 above; Georg Neumann: Page 6, 20, 24, 25, 26, 27, 28, 29, 30 31, 34, 35, 36, 37, 38, 39, 40, 41, 42, 43; Schumacher: Page 5, 7, 8, 9, 10, 11, 12, 13, 14, 15, 16, 21

Printed: R. Oldenbourg, Graphische Betriebe G. m. b. H., Munich